The Garage Sale Handbook

The Garage Sale Handbook

by Peggy Hitchcock

 Pilot Books

Published by
PILOT INDUSTRIES, INC.
P.O. Box 2102, Greenport, NY 11944-2102

1996 Edition

Library of Congress Catalog Card Number: 86-22532

Library of Congress Cataloging in Publication Data

Hitchcock, Peggy
   The garage sale handbook.

    1. Garage sales—handbooks, manuals, etc.
I. Title.
HF5482.3.H57   1986   658.8'7   86-22532
ISBN 0-87576-127-5

Printed in United States of America

ABOUT THE AUTHOR

Peggy Hitchcock is a garage sale expert who follows the same principles she applies as a successful corporation executive into the planning of a garage sale. She writes from practical experience.

In this endeavor she is assisted by her two children and an understanding husband.

CONTENTS

WHY THIS BOOK WAS WRITTEN

You've just picked up this book, and that means that you're seriously thinking about having a garage sale. Of course, it might also mean that you had a garage sale in the past, but you ended up with $33.25, sore feet and a terrible headache, and you're looking for help. Or maybe you're just looking for hints because you like to attend rather than give garage sales and you think this book might help. Well, in any of these cases, you're right. You will also be helped to decide whether a garage sale would be a good money-maker for you. Perhaps you're looking for information about how and when to set up a sale, plus what to charge. You want to know how to deal with the few obnoxious people who spend most of their waking weekend hours attending garage sales just to practice chiseling prices. The answers are here. And also the answers to questions you haven't even thought of yet. Here goes . . .

Chapter One

A Little Background

The word "garage" comes from a French word meaning to protect or preserve. The word "sale," of course, means the act of selling, exchange of property for an agreed sum of money; and also an opportunity to sell or be sold. So, a garage sale, by strictest definition, means selling things in a protected area. That covers a multitude of places. It could be held on a porch, in a basement, barn or attic. It could also be a sale not held in a protected area, such as a lawn, yard, or driveway. The reason for this variety of names for "garage sales" is to establish the physical location of where the sale is to be held. When folks drive up to your house, they'll know where to look. That is the only reason for the name change. In the newspaper's classified section, where you will want to place an ad about your sale, it will be placed under the heading of **"Garage Sales."** For the purpose of this book, we'll refer to this type of business as "garage sales" unless we're discussing the actual location of your sale, and advantages or disadvantages of the location.

First of all—and this is true in anything you attempt in life, be it the most humble effort of preparing a meal or a 25 year session of nuclear research—you must get in the proper frame of mind. Anyone, absolutely anyone, can put on a great garage sale. But it involves work and preparation, and you've got to accept that to begin with. There are no shortcuts to success, not even in the garage sale business. You've also got to have a strong desire to please the public. In order for your sale to be successful, you must measure up to what the customers expect. Because if they don't find what they expect at your sale, they'll just whip out their newspaper, mark you off, and continue on to another sale.

So, give it some thought, pump yourself up and get out your pencil and paper. Start making notes as you read along. Good luck!

Chapter Two

Proper Preparation

The most essential element of any project is proper organization. It means the difference between enjoying the event or taking an oath that, when it's all over, not only will you never have another garage sale, but you, and your children, and your children's children, will never attend another garage sale.

NEVER, NEVER plan a garage sale without allowing three weeks for preparation. Three weeks allows you time to have everything ready beforehand, so that you can relax and enjoy your sale.

The first thing on your preparation list is, do you require a permit for this sale? In some areas you will indeed need a permit and it will cost you a nominal amount. In most areas, however, no permit will be needed. Check with your local licensing bureau. If you aren't sure what agency handles this, call the mayor's office or local town hall and ask whom you call regarding a permit for a garage sale. They will tell you either that there is no need for the permit, or they will tell you whom to contact regarding the permit.

The second thing you must decide is the date on which you will hold the sale, and how many days it will last. As a rule, a three-day sale is best. A three-day sale allows you Friday, Saturday and Sunday to sell every item you wish to sell. If you work, of course you'll want to have it only on Saturday and Sunday. And, if you have less than 100 items to sell, you may want to have it only on Saturday. If you have a one-day sale, you can bet you'll probably be left with the very items you most sincerely hoped you'd never ever see again. The advantage of Saturday and Sunday is to allow other working people an opportunity to see your wares on their days off. Friday gives you that extra day of exposure, and you can be sure that the professional garage sale attenders will be there on Friday, and probably before opening time. So, in order of best choice, you have:

1) Friday, Saturday and Sunday
2) Saturday and Sunday
3) Saturday only

If you are planning to hold your sale in an unprotected area—
that is, yard, exposed patio, or the like—you may wish to choose a
"rain date" in case of a deluge or weather so bad you simply cannot
hold the sale. Rain dates are usually the same days on the following
weekend. You should remember to include the "rain date" in your
advertising.

Don't schedule your sale near a holiday. People are busy with
other things and you'll have a dreadfully small turnout. You may
want to avoid a weekend when there is a popular event going on in
your area. Read your newspaper and follow the local calendar of
events to make sure your customers are not somewhere else when
they should be at your house buying up all your treasures. This is
essential.

Some people will tell you to try to avoid having your garage sale
on the same days when many other people are having their sales.
That's rubbish. First of all, when people go out "garage sale-ing,"
they carry with them the Thursday night paper in which they have
carefully circled the most likely sounding sales. They are most apt
to be out and about when they can hit several sales in one trip. Also,
when they get to your sale, it will be so far superior to the other
sales they've seen, you'll be glad for the opportunity for your customers to compare your sale with the competition. Or if they call on
you first, they'll expect a lot from the next ones they try, probably
be disappointed and return later in the day to "have a little better
look" at your things.

So welcome the competition of other garage sales. You will certainly stand that test. You'll know you've got a winner going when
a customer chats a while with you, and after feeling comfortable,
confides that the other sales were "simply horrible" and "yours is
so nice and clean."

So, here's what to consider:

1) There are no major local events scheduled
2) Your next weekend is free in case of rainout
3) More garage sales bring out more people

Chapter Three

Selecting Your Location

Think carefully about where on your property you will hold your sale. There is much to consider before you jump into a location selection. Are your customers going to trample down your newly planted backyard grass? Is your garage so full of junk, there'll be no place to store your portable swimming pool and the outdoor grill? Can your porch support the weight of all those people? If you have a patio sale, will you tie up the only convenient entrance to your house? Do you really want people tramping through your kitchen to go to the cellar or basement? Think about each location systematically.

THE GARAGE. In order to have everything displayed in your garage, you've got to have some big garage. And an unfinished floor is no picnic to keep clean. If you have a two-car garage with a cement floor, and if there is easy access to it, this is the perfect place to have your sale—probably the best. You're going to have to remove everything you don't want sold, however, because invariably everyone is going to want to buy your brand new outdoor grill, and they're going to be upset because "Well, it's here! Why isn't it for sale?" This puts your customer in a bad mood, not conducive to buying. If it is absolutely impossible to remove some of the things that you are not planning to sell, stack them all together in the back, most inaccessible corner of your garage, and put a barrier in front of them. And we don't mean to hang a sheet in front of them. Kids (and adults) love to peek behind things, and that's like handing them an engraved invitation. So make sure all small things are removed from the garage and the big ones, if they must be there, are together and protected. Your best bet, of course, is just to pull everything that is not for sale out of the garage, haul it around to the back or store it elsewhere for the duration of the sale. It will avoid many possible problems. There is another great advantage to this. You've probably been wanting to clean out the garage and get rid of those things you don't use. But you don't because you are sure you are going to need them any time now. However, after starting to lug them out, you or your spouse may just change your mind and decide to "Go ahead and sell them. We'll probably never use them again anyhow." That gives you more merchandise and a clean garage. The advantages of a garage sale are endless.

Even though your garage is large, you still will probably have things that will have to be displayed outdoors. That's okay. Just be sure that the things outside are weather-resistant and fairly large so that you can keep an eye on them.

THE PATIO. This is a good place to have a sale. Most patios are covered either wholly or partially, allowing you to keep the perishables under cover. You can expand easily into the yard or driveway while still being able to keep your merchandise organized and displayed nicely. It is similar to the garage location, but chances are you won't have things stored in your patio area that have to be moved because they are not to be sold. It is also much cooler if the weather is hot. Since there are no boundaries (walls) to your patio, you'll need plenty of supervision to be sure everything is safe and secure.

THE YARD (OR BACKYARD). If you've got a good stand of grass, no prize flowers just pepping into bloom, and an undaunting optimism about the weather, have a yard sale. The room is endless; you can line up boxes and tables all over the place. You've got the same security problems as with the patio sale, however, and they're a little worse. Again, it's cooler than the garage. How about renting a big canopy-type tent like they use at outdoor wedding receptions from your local rent-all store? It protects you from the sun, and a little bit from the rain. Check out the cost though, unless your sale is a real biggie, because the rental charges will take a big bite out of your profits.

THE PORCH. We weren't kidding when we said to be sure the porch will support the weight of your customers. Most new houses don't have large porches, so if you've got one, chances are you have an older home. How's the porch holding up? Better check it out. You surely wouldn't want a prospective customer to lean against the railing and just keep right on going, over the side of the porch into your petunia patch. Porch sales are nice, but make sure your house is all cleaned up, because those same kids (and adults) who like to peek behind hanging sheets are going to peek in your windows. You will also want to be sure that the little ones don't go wandering into the house. Keep the doors and windows secured. When you need to go into the house, go around to the back door, unlock it and then lock it behind you. Porches are nice in case of a little bad weather, and screened porches will withstand a pretty hard rain without everything getting wet. Again, you can put items that won't be hurt by the rain on the areas beside the sidewalk leading up to the porch. Not a bad site selection.

THE BASEMENT (CELLAR). Unless you have a separate outside entrance to your basement, you are going to have your customers going through your house, probably your kitchen. If you don't mind, that's great. Lots of people do mind. We've had basement sales and never had a bit of problem with people coming into our home. As a matter of fact, some items of furniture we were selling were displayed in our family room upstairs. It all went well and we had no unhappy occurrences with it. We believe you will experience the same good things, but, as in any business and in any organization, you plan for the unexpected. An unhappy experience of someone's going into parts of your home where you do not want them is a possibility and you should plan what you are going to do if it should happen. If you live in the North, and are planning a sale in cold months, a basement sale is wonderful. It's much easier to store in an inaccessible section of the basement the things you normally keep in the basement but don't want to sell. You can hang clothes on your clothes lines for terrific viewing. Another good site selection.

THE BARN. If you have a working barn, your cows are going to be very upset with you if you have strangers poking around their home. And, too, it's probably a little smelly for some of your more urbane customers. Although I must say that I attended a barn sale where the cows stayed on their side of the barn and their owner held the sale on the other side. There was no problem with this because it was a farm community and we all knew what a barn smelled like. Even if you think you know who your potential customers will be, you're going to have some very elegantly dressed ladies come by and turn up their noses at the smell. If you're having your sale in a barn, you've got to believe that these ladies could read and, therefore, knew it was in a barn. So, let the shopper beware. If your barn is just an empty building on your property, all clean and nice with no friendly creatures living in it, you may have such a wonderful place for a barn sale, you'll want to go into the business. We'll talk more about this later.

THE ATTIC. Attic sale usually does not mean that the sale is being held in an attic. Most folks don't have attics suitable for a sale. It means that the items in the sale come from the attic.

The preferred selection for sale sites are:

1) Nice, big, clean garage
2) Nice, big, clean basement/cellar
3) Airy, covered patio
4) Big, sturdy porch
5) Grassy, fenced backyard
6) Big, clean barn (wouldn't be last on our list if we thought more people had them)

Whenever possible, utilize covered and closed areas—even if they aren't as cool—if your sale will last longer than one day.

So now you've set your sale date and decided where you're actually going to hold the sale, i.e., garage, basement, yard, etc. You're now ready to start telling your friends and neighbors about it. Be ready for the horror stories. Take them with a grain of salt. Hopefully you will hear a lot of very positive things, mostly how much money was raised, which is, if not the most important, certainly ranking right up there with the good reasons for holding the sale.

"Hey, I'm having a garage sale on Friday, Saturday and Sunday, the 8th, 9th and 10th. Be sure to tell everyone and be sure to come!" That's the spirit. You're on the right track.

Chapter Four

Advertising Your Sale

There are several ways to let the world know that you're having a sale. Word-of-mouth is very, very good, but hardly enough. The newspaper is probably most effective, because garage sale-ing has become a hobby for a lot of people and they watch for the ads in the newspapers. It's how they spend their weekends. They've gotten very sophisticated about it.

Thursday night seems to be the prime time to start your ad. Run it Thursday, Friday and Saturday. If you want to limit your expenditure on the ad and cut down on the number of days you run your ad, put it in Thursday's paper for sure. That's the one more people use when they sit down to circle likely prospects.

Although people are probably drawn to read a particularly long classified ad in the garage sale category simply to see what in the world anyone could say about a garage sale that took up so much space, you really need only a few items of information. Name of *sale:* Basement Sale, or whatever kind of sale it is; *Days of the week:* Friday, Saturday, Sunday (you can abbreviate); *Dates:* 8th, 9th, 10th of August; Time: 10 a.m. til 6 p.m., or even 10 til 6; and *a general idea of what you are offering for sale.* One of our favorite lines for what's being sold at a garage sale is "lots of everything." That surely covers it. If you have furniture or large appliances, be sure to mention that in the ad. Serious buyers who need those types of things are looking for them in garage sale ads.

Do consider the delivery time of your newspaper and adjust accordingly. Morning delivery means advertise on Friday morning, rather than Thursday morning. Some newspapers deliver in the evenings on weekdays and mornings on weekends. So if your sale is Friday, Saturday and Sunday, you'd get the most coverage with Thursday evening, Friday evening and Saturday morning. If you have morning delivery every day of the week and your sale is on Saturday only, or Saturday and Sunday only, still start the ad on Friday and continue it Saturday. Most people feel they don't benefit a lot from running the ad on Sunday, even if their sale is going to run on Sunday. And don't make the mistake we've noticed several times of advertising in a Sunday paper when your sale ended on Saturday.

Here are some examples of ads we feel attracted more attention than the run-of-the-mill garage sale ad:

Patio Sale! Everything under the sun from 25¢ to $100. Furniture too. Fri., Sat., Sun., from 10 til 6. Rain date next week same time. 125 Main Street.

Yard Sale. Fri., Sat. only. 10 til 6. Lots of everything. Treasures of three families. Refreshments sold. Next week same time if it rains. 125 Main Street.

Garage Sale. Saturday and Sunday from 10 til 6. Toys, dishes, clothing, books, plus much more. Rain or shine. 125 Main Street.

The first ad tells people that there will be things there of value ($100) so be sure that's what you mean. Again, "furniture" will attract many people who might otherwise not have come. The second ad tells your potential customers that you're sure to have a big selection because three families pooled all their stuff. Also, "refreshments sold" attracts those folks who make a day of it. They'll have a snack at your place. The third ad is fairly standard—gives a touch of what you'll be selling. Many, many people look for old dishes and glassware. Lots of people are book buffs and you've tantalized them a bit with your ad. Don't forget "rain date." Again, be sure next weekend is clear. Is Aunt Grace coming for her annual visit? Does Billy plan to have the Scout Troop over for a full-day picnic on Saturday? Be sure to check it out.

Note that we didn't have to put a rain date in the garage sale ad, because the garage is big enough that, even if it rains, you'll be able to go through with the sale. By putting "rain or shine" in your ad, if it should rain, the weekend garage sale-ers who thought they were out of luck will flock to your house. You never have a weather problem with a basement or barn sale with the exception of a hurricane, a tornado, or two feet of snow.

For your newspaper ad, because you've got a three-week preparation period, you will have plenty of time to call your newspaper's classified ad department and ask about costs, etc. The three sample ads ranged in length from 22 to 28 words. Count your words before you call. Find out exactly what time you must have your ad in their hands in order to get it in the paper on the days you want. Don't just get the date or day, find out what time, too. All you need to spoil the works is to walk in Wednesday afternoon at 3:00 p.m., ad clutched in your hand, to find that you had to be there by 2:30. Half an hour means a lot in the newspaper business. Everything is ready for the sale on Friday, but nobody is going to know about it. So be sure of your deadline for placing the ad.

While you're chatting with the people at the newspaper, ask if they have any kind of public service section where they list community events, garage sales included, free of charge. Some newspapers do that. If they say "yes," be sure they understand that yours is a private sale and not connected with any charitable organization—although your spouse will probably give you an argument on that point.

Okay, now you've taken care of word-of-mouth and newspaper advertisement. Don't overlook the real freebies of advertising—bulletin boards in grocery stores, discount stores, libraries, churches and schools. On 3x5 cards, print up the same type of information as you have in your newspaper ad. Make sure you put the date as well as the day of the week, because these cards will go up several days or possibly a week or more before your sale. Carry these cards around with you, and as you go into a store that has a bulletin board, tack up your ad. If you live in a college town, a sale held the latter part of August or early September will bring out the kids who opted for an apartment rather than the dorm. They need all kinds of things like you are selling, and they need them cheap. Make sure they know about your sale.

Never underestimate the power of advertising. Clever advertising gives you the edge over everyday, humdrum signs and cards. On your 3x5 cards, add a bright, colorful decoration—a flower or a sketch of a garage—some little something that will catch the eye of the person glancing at the bulletin board.

Advertising Checklist:

1) **Find out the newspaper schedule—when your ad must be in.**
2) **Write an ad that fits your sale**
3) **Make up your 3x5 cards for bulletin boards**
4) **Tell everyone you know about your sale**
5) **March down to the newspaper and hand them your ad—and your check.**

You're swinging now. Oh, no. Now comes the hard physical work.

SIGN MAKING

Several days before your sale, sit down and make a list of the signs you'll need. First of all, you need a sign for the front of your house which simply says "Garage Sale" or "Patio Sale" or whatever. If you live in an area that is difficult to find, you may want to make several small signs which say "Garage Sale—125 Main Street" and add an arrow showing which direction to drive. It is essential, if you plan to post these kinds of signs along the route to your home on telephone poles, etc., that you check with your local government agency in charge of that sort of thing. You can ask about it when you call about a permit. You'd be terrifically embarrassed if, right in the middle of your sale, a policeman drives up with all your signs in his hand and wonders in a deep voice "Who's in charge of this garage sale?"

Be sure to remove all signs after your sale is over.

You'll need signs for your refreshment stand if you are going to have one.

You'll need signs advertising the fact that at a certain time on one of the days of your sale, you are going to reduce your prices.

You might want a "Closed" sign.

Have you ever attended a garage sale and, upon arriving at the house, find a haphazardly cut piece of brown cardboard with "garage sale" scribbled across it in pencil? Did you get the feeling that this whole sale was a last minute idea? Make sure you don't give that impression. Make your signs neat, cheerful and easy to read. Don't make them so involved that they are difficult to decipher. Just say what you need to say. Plan what you are going to say. Don't compose as you go along, or you will be writing up the side and down the back, and your printing will get smaller and smaller.

Your largest sign will be the one in your front yard and you will want it to be bright and noticeable. We suggest poster board which you can purchase at most discount department stores, stationery stores or office supply stores. They are big enough to do the job, and come in a variety of colors. We suggest white or yellow. Get a good, wide-tipped black felt marker for your main lettering and a few other colors for your trim and decorations. Have tape and tacks on hand.

Determine how large you want your front yard sign to be. If you want to use a whole poster board, that's fine, but you'll have to put a backing on it, because poster is too flimsy to hold in any kind of breeze. Use the side of a large cardboard box for backing. You can tape or staple the poster board to the cardboard and have a very sturdy sign. You'll need a proper stake for the sign unless you have a tree or mailbox, strategically located right on the street, on which you can attach the sign. If you place your sign so that it faces the street, you'll need only one sign. If you place it so that it can be read as your customers drive up from either direction, you will need two signs, fitted back to back, facing each direction of the street. That's really the better way to do it.

On your poster boards, pencil in the wording, and after you are pleased with the positioning of the letters, trace over the penciled letters with your marker. Make sure the letters are easy to read—not too fancy. Make them good and wide without running into each other. You may want to add the hours (10 til 6) at the bottom of your sign. Make those letters smaller. Then be sure to add your decorative and colorful designs around the border to make the sign eye-catching. First impressions count, and this is the customer's first impression of your sale. Make it a good one.

Get creative with your refreshment stand sign. If coffee is free, say so. If snacks cost 25¢, say that, too. Add a little design or decoration to keep up with your sign out front.

Make sure you have your signs about upcoming price reductions, and 25% off, and 50% off signs prepared and ready. Decorate these signs with stars and lightning zig-zags to show they're explosive material. Use your imagination. Put your kids to work on ideas.

Chapter Five

Selecting Your Merchandise

If you've been the head or co-head of a household and never had a garage sale, it tells us something very interesting about your personality. You are most likely a saver. Horrors! This garage sale exercise may prove a very hard experience for you. In order to get in the right frame of mind for selecting items to go into your sale, you may have to resort to extreme measures. You're probably essentially a good-natured person, even-tempered and sentimental. You will have a terrible time deciding to part with things that have been a part of your life for a while.

Try this. You are looking at a tie rack your husband made with his own hands. He slaved for weeks on it. He has never, ever used it. Remember that cutting remark he made about your mother's apple pie? Wham. Into the garage sale box it goes. Golf shoes? He hasn't golfed for years—they probably wouldn't fit him anyway. How about that time you stood freezing in front of the movie theater for 45 minutes waiting for him to pick you up while he sat at home, warm and cozy, watching a football game. Thump. Into the box. This is little Billy's favorite Tonka toy. But wait a minute. Billy is fifteen years old now. And remember that he hasn't made his bed once in those fifteen years. Kaboom. Another one for the box. In this manner you can harden yourself into putting almost anything that you or a member of your family hasn't really wanted or used in the last year into the dreaded garage sale box.

You may have more problems when it comes to things you have cherished over the years. Convince yourself that if in the future you really need a fish-shaped serving platter, you'll just go out and buy yourself another one. And, really, if miniskirts come back in fashion for us older girls, we'd probably look silly in them anyhow.

Try to gather all your merchandise together in one session and get it over with. Don't change your mind. Once it's in the box, don't take it out. Don't let anyone con you into keeping something that you know in your heart no one will be able to use. Show no mercy.

Don't feel embarrassed about putting things in your sale that you think are silly. Everyone has different tastes. Something that you hate may be just what someone else has been searching for for two years. And something that you really felt bad about putting into the sale because you loved it, may not interest a single person coming to your sale. In essence, don't try to guess what people will want. Simply put out everything you don't use and want to be rid of. Someone will be delighted with it.

Another good rule to follow is "if no one has used it or even asked for it in the past year, it's ready for a garage sale." Even if it is an expensive crock pot in mint condition, if you don't ever use it, you don't need it. And if you haven't used it in a year, odds are that you will never use it again. You have three lovely glass pitchers. All are in the attic. They are in the attic because you don't have use for them. The only things that you should keep in your attic are things that are stored there because they are used seasonally. Other than papers and documents which must be kept, everything in your attic theoretically should go into your sale. That's true of the basement, too. Or the storage room. And check your sewing room. Go into the very top of your kids' closets. Insist that the kids go through their things for garage sale candidates. Reason with them. Be firm, and don't neglect the garage itself.

If you've been planning to replace your kitchen table in the fall, and it's already August, sell it at your garage sale. It's the perfect time, and a real customer-puller. If you wait to get rid of it until you actually purchase your new table, you'll be stuck with it. The store where you purchase the new one will most likely not give you a trade-in, and used furniture dealers laugh when you call and tell them you have just one item to sell. Even if they come out to see the table, they'll offer you a fraction of what you will be able to get at your sale. Remember, they have to mark up their price from your price to make a profit and pay overhead.

Sometimes when you've moved into a house, the last owner will have left junk there for you, rather than going to the trouble of hauling it away. You may not recognize most of it. Now's your chance to get rid of it. Add it to your sale. If you don't know what it is, stack it all together under a sign reading "Whatchamacallits."

Other things you might overlook when you are searching for merchandise are: luggage, toys, books, tools, Christmas ornaments, pictures, and kitchen items.

Chapter Six

Preparing Your Merchandise

Now that you have accumulated everything you are going to offer at your sale, clean it up. This is the one most important thing you will do to increase profits dramatically. You will sell 100% more than your neighbor with the same quality and amount of items, if you simply take the time to wash those glasses and make them sparkle. Dust those books. Wipe the old ones with a vinegar-water saturated cloth if they have a mildew odor. Make sure they smell nice. Old tools? Take your Brillo pad to them. A little Pledge on a rag will brighten up wooden handles. Did you find some old clay garden pots? Clean off all the mud and dirt. They'll look like new. You can charge at least twice as much for items well displayed and clean, in good repair, than the same items just as you took them from wherever you found them. This is your "one up" on others. People will simply not take the time nor make the effort to properly prepare items for sale.

This preparation will take some time, but you're having this sale with the main purpose of making money, aren't you? This will do it.

Don't be too quick to throw away cracked dishes. Some people repair old china and pottery as a hobby. Or the dish, even though it is cracked may be so pretty that someone will buy it as a planter for ivy. Even if your dishes and glassware are cracked or have a chip out of the rim, make them shine. Put your kids to work on this.

Let's talk a minute about what you're going to display at your sale. Dishes are excellent sellers. Glassware seems to be in demand if nothing else is selling. People collect bottles. One word of warning. We are not antique experts. You probably are not, either. Play it safe. The U.S. Customs Service defines antiques as anything at least 100 years old. So does the dictionary. Go a little further. If you know that an item is over 50 years old, don't sell it. If you don't know, but suspect that it is over 50 years old and is in good repair, don't sell it. It is difficult to determine if you have a valuable item, but now is not the time to spend on finding out. Just put those items in a box and store them away until you can investigate thoroughly. Remember, over 50 years—keep it. We'll talk more about antiques later in the book.

Furniture sells well. If it is not in good condition, those kids from the local college couldn't care less. They'll use it anyway. Wooden furniture with a broken this-or-that can be repaired by someone who likes to do that sort of thing, then refinished and made into a very respectable piece. Put it out for sale.

DO NOT ATTEMPT TO HIDE OR CONCEAL THE FACT THAT SOMETHING IS NOT WORKING. Be honest no matter what. If you don't sell it, at least you'll be able to sleep at night. If it is totally a lost cause, trash it. Don't waste valuable display space with items that will not sell simply because they have absolutely no value at all.

Be sure appliances and electrical things work. Try them out, push the buttons, flip the levers. Let them run a minute to be sure they don't set themselves on fire. Note: Even if your toaster oven, or whatever, does not work, if it is still in reasonable shape, sell it—with the clear stipulation that it is not working and will need to be repaired. Tape a slip of paper on the side saying "Doesn't work—needs repairs." Be sure that the buyer understands that the item is broken and that you cannot be responsible for it. If they buy it, they buy it as-is and you cannot take it back if they find it turned out to be a bad deal. You are selling this item for almost nothing anyhow, because it doesn't work, so even if it cannot be repaired, the buyer is not out much, and might have the deal of the century. I know a couple who bought a non-working Sony Trinitron 21 inch T.V. for $5.00, had it repaired for $65.00, and now have a wonderful television set.

If you spend 10 minutes thoroughly cleaning that mixer, you are sure to realize $2 to $3 more than if it's caked with Bisquick and has that black grease around the base. That averages out to $12 to $18 an hour for your labor. Really, it's going to pay off and then some. Again I implore you, if you have kids, put them to work. They're usually just hanging around the house with nothing to do and complaining bitterly about it.

Knickknacks always sell well if they aren't too expensive. Candlesticks need to be polished. Remember to make sure you are not selling your sterling. Or perhaps you want to sell, but remember that it's sterling when it comes time to price it.

Clothes, clothes, clothes. These are frequently a drudge on the market. I think it may be a pride thing. Someone is reluctant to buy even a lovely silk dress that would fit well and costs almost nothing if they think their friends would know they bought it second-hand. But then, people from the neighboring town may come by and snap it up. So it's a maybe situation. But don't neglect to put out your nicest in-good-shape clothing at your sale. In depressed economic times, it sometimes becomes necessary for many people to select used clothing. It is certainly no sin—and really a smart move on the buyer's part. Some well-off people get a kick out of a real buy in clothing. Wash every item that can be washed. If it needs to be dry-cleaned, you may think twice before having that done. The cost of the cleaning may be more than you will make on the sale of the item. Clothes usually sell very cheaply. Again, we'll talk about pricing later.

You pull out a dress that went out of style 30 years ago and worse than that, it has a huge stain down the side. It is totally unsalvageable. Except for those uniquely beautiful buttons. There are eight of them. Snip them off and tape them to one of your leftover 3x5 cards. The same with that old sweater. It has twelve matching buttons. How about that 15 inch zipper in the dress you just snipped the buttons from? If you can remove good, usable zippers from old, unusable clothes without too much effort, simply by "ripping," do it. Put them in your "Sewing Corner" section of your sale. Old patterns sell, too, but make sure all the pieces are there. Throw in those half skeins of yarn. As we said before, go through your sewing material. Have you given up knitting or crocheting? Sell your needles, hooks and pattern books. If you're keeping them for old age, don't. Probably by the time you're older, you'll be heavily into cross-country skiing.

Lampshades sell well. Clean them up first. Do you have every "Better Homes and Gardens" since 1955? Have you looked at one since you put them in that box? Tell the truth now. Put them in your book section. Old towels, washcloths, and linens sell. But be sure they are perfectly clean and sweet smelling. We don't mean to perfume them. Just make sure they smell good and clean. Blankets are good sellers.

People don't normally have a full set of tableware to sell at a garage sale—usually just stray forks and spoons that don't match. If you have this kind of an array of eating utensils and really don't use them, put it out. Folks use this kind of thing at summer homes or on boats, or even in picnic baskets. We just slipped in a hint for the garage sale buyer.

We have a college student daughter. Every time she comes home and goes back to school, l can't find a hanger in the house. If you've got millions of them clogging up your closets, take good ones, neatly band them together in big bunches, 15 or 20, and put them out for sale. Maybe someone like me will come along and need hangers; or maybe they have some wonderful invention that requires hangers. Even if they don't sell, they are now neatly packed together for easy disposal.

It is impossible to figure out why people buy what they do at garage sales. Don't try. Just put out everything you have, clean, neat and in good condition. It will sell.

Don't sell—we repeat—don't sell half-used jars of food. You may think this is a strange thing to put in this book, but we actually attended a sale where the folks giving the sale had put out half-used up jars of pickles. Now I don't know but that could be against the law. And it if isn't, it should be.

Big pieces of carpeting, sometimes even those in pretty bad shape, will sell. Someone may be using it to carpet their dog house, make throw carpets for in front of their washer and dryer in the basement, or maybe they want to re-carpet their car trunk. Odd curtains, perhaps even just half a pair, can sell. Cookie cutters, slotted spoons, serving pieces of the kitchen variety, all sell well, as do pots and pans. Get busy with that Brillo pad. Double your money.

Old-fashioned coffee pots will sell to campers, or to someone who has a stove in the basement. They can keep a pot of coffee going while they iron. If your fancy new coffee pot with the clock and timer has gone kaput, sell it with the "not working—needs repairs" sign on it. Someone may want it just for the clock and timer, which still work fine.

Take time to examine the toys you are putting out for sale. Make sure they are really salable and not in need of repair. Some little one may spy something you are selling and be heartbroken if they can't have it because it isn't safe. It isn't sanitary to sell non-washable stuffed animals that have been chewed on by your kids, no matter how clean you kept them (the animals, that is). If you're selling puzzles, be a sport and indicate that there are 2 pieces missing, if they are. A real puzzler won't be deterred if he or she likes the puzzle, but it's dirty pool to let them search for days for a piece that doesn't exist. (Shoppers, you can pick up those fabulous Springbok puzzles at a fraction of their price at garage sales if you get there early). Beware if you ever visit our house for a sale. Our dogs have eaten at least one piece of every puzzle we've ever had.

Coloring books that children outgrew before they colored more than a few pages, crayons with the points just barely dulled, puzzle books never touched, all these are real finds for little ones. They enjoy this kind of surprise better than the brand new ones from the store, just because they discovered it themselves while Mom and Dad were sorting through a stack of books.

If we promised you that we could double your profits at a garage sale with just three words, those words would be "MAKE EVERY-THING SHINE." Use them and you'll be well on your way to achieving your goal. We cannot stress too much the value of proper preparation of your sale items.

Now you're ready for pricing.

Chapter Seven

Pricing Your Merchandise

Pricing is usually regarded as the hardest part of a garage sale. If it presents problems for you, we'll attempt to soothe your fears. Some of the dread should have been removed simply by requesting that you not attempt to sell anything that could possibly be antique and valuable. Using the 50 years or older rule will not always save you. Comic books from the forties are very valuable. You've just got to feel that you've taken reasonable precautions, and if someone buys something from you that is worth $10,000, it must be fate.

Be assured that there is no absolute right or wrong in pricing items for sale at a garage sale. Everyone in the whole world, amateur and expert alike, prices some items too high, some too low, and hits on the right price about one time in ten. So don't be paranoid about marking your things. Keep one thing in mind. Items such as pots and pans, everyday glassware, and items which most people use every day and really have need for, can be priced much higher than a knickknack that someone buys on a lark.

Knickknacks, unless they are home-made craft items and really nice, don't bring a big price. Let's face it. If it were something you really liked, you wouldn't be selling it anyway. Price it accordingly. Always remember that philosophy regarding garage sales. You are never selling anything you really want to keep. On the contrary, you are selling things you really don't want or need, with the object of making extra money. Look at it in a business-like manner as a potential moneymaker, with the goal of clearing as much profit as possible.

You don't want to end up a mental patient over the issue of pricing. Sometimes two heads are better than one if you are feeling wishy-washy about pricing. Ask a good friend, a really good friend, to come over and help you. Bear one thing in mind. Even though you don't want an item at this time, you probably selected and bought it sometime in the past, or it was given to you as a gift by someone you love, so even though you are getting rid of it now, you have some fond memory of it. You may get your feelings royally hurt if your best friend laughs and wonders who in the world would have bought this ridiculous thing, and suggests that you don't even have to put a price on it, because it will never sell. So thicken your skin. You might as well get in practice, because you will likely hear more of these kinds of comments at the sale itself. And remember, you asked. Your friend didn't volunteer.

If you and your friend are miles apart as to what value an item should have, agree to go half way between each value and mediate the price. You won't be much more wrong than if you stayed at either end of the price range. You'll probably have more laughs over this pricing business with your friend than you've had in years. Garage sales, even the preparation part, are tremendous fun if you relax and enjoy them.

In pricing, a good rule that we have used successfully in the past is the "20% rule." If you sell an item in reasonably good shape for 20% of the price you originally paid for it, you will be arriving at a pretty fair price. If an item is in really fine condition, you can push that percentage up to 25% and maybe 30%—or more. You will be able to judge after you have priced a dozen or so pieces. If you don't feel comfortable with this formula, go around to a few garage sales several weeks before you have yours. We think you'll be convinced. Some people price their items ridiculously low; some unrealistically high. You'll be just about right. But not for clothes.

As we said, clothes are usually hard to sell. We attended a garage sale given by a church in Ohio. They had a beautiful fuzzy, long sleeved clean sweater in super condition for sale at 10¢. All dresses were 50¢ and all suits, 75¢. We spotted an Evan Picone suit for 75¢. Coats were $2. A sweater that you bought 5 years ago would probably have cost $30. The 20% rule would have you ask $6 for the sweater. We don't think you'd get it. Maybe, but probably not. There may be another solution for this on your last day of the sale—"drastic price reductions." We'll discuss that later.

Another source for pricing is a recent Sears catalogue. Look up what electric knives are selling for, use the 20% rule and mark your product. If you prove us wrong by studying other sales, adjust your prices accordingly so that you feel comfortable with them. But then, like the old man said, maybe we're right and the rest of the world is wrong.

A stove that cost $300 five years ago might be worth more than $60 to $100, but don't forget this is a garage sale, and people who are shopping for appliances (as-is) at a garage sale are buying with no guarantee of any kind. They're looking for bargains and they're taking their chances that the entire insides of the stove won't drop out as they remove it from their truck at home. So give 'em a break. If they wanted to pay $200 for that stove, they'd go to a used furniture place where they'd at least get a 90-day guarantee. You should NOT guarantee these things. You're selling honestly and presenting the items as fairly as possible. You cannot and must not do more than that. You'll be in a world of trouble if you do. As usual, we have an exception to this. We sold phonograph records—albums—which we'd had for years and which few people would have liked. No great bargains—the 20% rule—$1 each. One little lady came and selected five or six. She asked if they all were in good condition and playable. I truthfully said I didn't know because they hadn't been played for years, but if she took them home and any didn't play, she could come back and swap (no refunds) for whatever records were left. She went away pleased. She came back the next day with two records and said they skipped. She happily picked two others, and then she bought a few more items. We'll bet she would have come back to any garage sale we'd have had in the future. We made a friend for life, at least for a garage sale life. So if you can make a suggestion like this for something the customer wants to try at home, do it. But don't ever put yourself in the position of having to refund money, or having to trade "up" on an item. This is not Sears Roebuck, you know. And if they are coming back to trade, they must come during garage sale hours. When the sale is over, so is their opportunity to trade.

With regard to physically marking your merchandise as you determine the prices, you should purchase some self-adhesive peel-off labels. Mark your price on the label and affix it to your item. Then do one more thing. Take a piece of chalk and mark that same price on the item in some other place. When the customers bring you the items they want to buy, you remove the label and stick it in your garage sale record book. This way you will have a permanent record of what monies you should have in your cash box at the end of the day. Because if the label is in your book, you have definitely sold the item. There is no chance of mistaken charges because the labels are mysteriously switched from one item to another. As you take the label off the item, you check to see that it matches the chalked price on the item. Sometimes the labels fall off. If they do, you won't have to guess what the label said. Check the chalked price and you're swinging. It will save you a great deal of trouble on sale day, and every problem you take care of in advance makes the sale more pleasurable for you.

Since we've started to talk about your garage sale record book, we'll mention here that record keeping schedules, etc. will be discussed later.

If you want to be very efficient and really get into record keeping, assign each item an item number as you make your label. Then enter both the item number and the price on your label. In a separate book, list item number and a very brief description of the item, and the cost you have assigned to it. Later on, when you are reviewing the results of your sale, you'll be able to determine what sold for how much, and you will have an excellent source for pricing for your next sale.

If you have 45 miscellaneous knives, forks and spoons, and don't want to mark each one individually, just put them in a nice, flat box, so your customers can sort through them easily without messing up everything around them, and put a sign on the box saying 10¢ each (or whatever price you determine for them). At your cash table where you will be sitting and keeping your records and cash box—and which no one leaves unattended for even one second—have a price list for items not individually marked. Then when someone is sitting in for you minding the cash station, they won't have any problem with prices.

Chapter Eight

Displaying Your Merchandise

Take time to map out, on paper, how you want to set up your wares. Always group your items together by category. Earlier on we mentioned "Sewing Center." You'll also probably be able to have "Book Shelves" where you will want to include magazines and periodicals as well as hard back and paper back books. "Kitchen Stuff" is self-explanatory, and includes pots, pans and utensils. Make your dishes and glassware a category of their own. You'll get a lot of traffic in that area. Also it's mostly breakable and you will want to be sure it is properly set up.

Clothes, of course, should be hung on hangers on a clothes line, unless you happen to have a portable clothes rack. If you stack clothes in a pile on a table, the same thing will happen to them that happens to a sale table at a department store. Things get tangled up, unfolded and some land on the floor. So as far as possible, even if you have to pin the things on hangers with safety pins, hang them up.

Don't forget your "Whatchamacallit Box." Put anything you are not sure of in this area.

Make sure anything electrical that you are selling is located near an electrical outlet so that you can demonstrate that it works. Make use of your manpower when setting up. If you've got a teenage daughter, she may really get into arranging displays. Sometimes these kids are so talented, it's amazing.

Don't put a bunch of things in a box on the floor. You've got three weeks before the sale. Ask the man at the supermarket to save you some large cartons. Take them home, set two of them upside down and tape them together. Now you've got a fairly good-sized display table. Also, if you are a good member of your church or synagogue, you might be able to borrow one or two of their big folding tables. These are terrific. Friends may lend you their metal folding tables they aren't using that weekend. Ask. They'll more than likely help you out. But they won't know you need something unless you ask.

If you are selling small items of costume jewelry or coins, which, although not priceless, are more expensive items, you may wish to keep them under glass. You can achieve this by asking the grocery man for a flat box, approximately 18 x 12 x 4 inches high. Sometimes peaches come in this type of box. Line the bottom of the box with cloth, arrange your small items in the box and lay a piece of glass over it. If you have a sterna window from a small bathroom or kitchen window, that will work well. It might even cover two of these boxes. If you don't have storm windows, you will have to think of something else. Maybe the local glass and windshield company will give you a piece of glass that didn't fit when they cut it for a job. Be sure to tape the edges of the glass heavily in order to avoid cut fingers—yours and your customers'. It is worth fussing like this because it relieves your mind of that worry about someone's picking up something without paying for it. We say, as we've said in the past, most people are very, very honest. You might happen on the odd person. Better to be safe than sorry. Also you're taking away temptation by covering up this kind of stuff.

FAITHFUL CO-WORKERS

Never, never hold a garage sale unless you have someone you can depend upon fully to spend the entire day with you, helping. Think about this. If nothing else, you'll have to go to the bathroom some-time during the day, and sure enough, if there is no one in sight and you think you can sneak away for three minutes, it's as though the customers have been lurking behind trees waiting for you to leave. They'll descend on your place en masse, waving money and asking questions. You'll never get away.

You also need someone for security and to mingle with the cus-tomers and answer their questions. You need to be able to trade off—someone to watch the money box and records while you take time to visit with the customers. That's half the fun. Also, when things get slow, the extra person can slip into the house and bring out a sand-wich to share with you.

Two extra people are not too many, especially if you are having a large sale. Anything longer than a one-day sale is a large sale. Do not use kids under 15 as your main helpers. For some reason, people tend to ignore them. And it's a shame that people treat these great young folks that way, but they do. Don't get us started on that subject, or we'll fill several chapters on that subject alone. We'll say no more at this point than don't use the younger kids.

If you have children under 6 years, be sure to farm them out for the day. They think they will enjoy being at the garage sale with you, and they think they'll have lots and lots of fun and be lots of help, but, really, they won't. They'll be bored and needing attention from you just when you are your busiest. Let them stay for half an hour, give them explicit instructions that they are just to watch for that half hour, they are not to question you or offer comments, and then they're off to Aunt Beverly's for the day. Believe me, no matter how much you usually give in to your kids, you're going to be sorry if you do it this time. You may even want to raise that age limit to 12. At 12, most kids can be a real help to you and get real satisfaction out of being needed. Don't be so nervous about your sale that you get short with them or make them feel bad. They may turn out to be the best, most reliable help you've got.

Do you have pets? By all means, farm them out, too. Nothing is more distracting than to have a dog barking in the basement or behind some locked door. Or worse yet, sniffing around your customers' feet. And nothing is more offensive to cat-haters than to have a cat rubbing around their legs. (We ourselves are cat-lovers, so don't write letters.) Take care of these arrangements well in advance and be sure to call the pet-babysitter the night before so they don't forget and happen to be off for the day, leaving you with a real live problem.

SUPPLIES FOR THE SALE

The minute you begin to prepare for your sale, start saving bags and boxes for your customers to carry out their buys. Those plastic bags the grocery stores are using now are terrific for this. Ask your friends and neighbors to save them for you. Remind them a couple of times. It's easy to forget when you aren't directly involved in a project .

How many workers are you going to have at your sale? Well, there is you, of course, and one or two friends who are going to help, and Billy and his friend who are going to run the refreshment stand. When you think about it, all you workers will look very much like the customers. Why not get (or make) five aprons so you all match and anyone who needs help will be able to pick out the workers from the customers. We'll bet even good old Billy won't mind wearing one. If need be, you can make aprons from colorful crepe paper. Or if aprons don't appeal to you, how about rounding up five matching-color baseball hats, use your poster board scraps to make bands for them which read "Garage Sale

Official" or "I'm Management—Ask me" or some phrase to indicate to the customers whom they can ask questions of or get help from.

Your cash box, or boxes, if you are having a refreshment stand and charging for snacks, need not be more than a cigar box. It certainly doesn't have to have a lock or be anything special. The reason for this is that the box will never be more than a foot from you and your eyes. And, please, don't violate this rule.

Of course you'll need to round up a table and chair for your cash box station. You'll want a few other chairs for the coworkers because you will go through lull periods when no one—not a single customer—will be on the premises.

You might want to keep a tape measure handy on the cash station table. Someone will probably want to measure a little table to see if it will fit between the refrigerator and the cupboard, and will have forgotten to bring their own tape.

A package of wet wipes always saves the day. If not fancy wet wipes, at least keep a box of Kleenex around. You should also have two pens on your table to keep your record book up to the minute, because one pen will invariably be under the table just when you need it.

A supply of scrap paper and a couple of pencils come in handy in case a customer wants to jot down something you have but they can't decide upon. They may think it over and come back. Noting your name and address on a piece of paper will remind them at which garage sale they saw the item.

Have a couple of chairs at your refreshment stand for customers. Grandma and Grandpa might enjoy resting their feet, sipping coffee and eating a brownie. They'll then be refreshed and able to fight their way back into the crowds and buy, buy, buy.

If you're not too swift at math, keep a little calculator on your cash station table so that you can quickly figure what an item would cost if it were reduced 25%. We'll not attempt a math course right here in the middle of this book, but the easiest way to do it is, for a 25% reduction, enter the original cost of the item, hit the multiply button, then enter .75. This will give you a 25% reduction of the original price. For a 50% reduction, enter the original cost, multiply button, and then .5. That'll give you a 50% reduction. If you have to go to a 75% reduction, enter the original price, multiply button, then enter .25, and that gives you a 75% reduction of the original price. Trust me.

Supplies for your refreshment stand, if you choose to have one, follow in the next section.

Chapter Nine

Refreshments

If you have planned to have a pot of coffee going at your sale, and that's a very nice idea, be sure you have a good supply of paper cups, little stirring sticks, and those tiny packages of sweetener and creamer so you don't have to fuss. A teenager can be in charge of the coffee pot. If you don't have a teenager of your own, enlist one of the neighborhood kids. Pay a nominal fee for this help. That fee you'll have to decide for yourself. It should, however, be enough to make them want to come and stay the day.

A snack concession also goes over well at a garage sale, and is a possible money-maker for the kids. Let them buy a couple of packages of brownie mix and/or cookie mix, turn them loose in the kitchen and let them create. Advance them the money to buy the supplies, but keep track of it and deduct it from their profits. We suggest any type of sweet that can be handled well from a napkin and does not require plate or fork.

The kids should have their own cash box so that they can keep track of how much they make, after, of course, paying you back for what they owe for supplies. Don't forget to have change on hand for their cash box, too. They'll have to return it to you. Stress to them the absolute necessity of keeping someone at their cash box at all times.

At this point, you now have free coffee, and cookies or brownies at a reasonable price. You might want to include lemonade or iced tea on your menu, also free like the coffee, or you may want to charge for it. That's a decision between you and the kids.

Don't forget to have a trash basket handy for discarded cups and napkins.

Your snack concession should have its own sign. Be sure to advertise what is free and what you are charging for. Make it a bright, colorful sign. Let the kids do it, but be sure everyone can read it.

Chapter Ten

Security

Taking measures to make sure your sale is properly protected is just good sense, and must be taken seriously.

If you are in charge of the cash box, stay there. If a customer needs help, stay where you are and either point out another "Garage Sale Official" or call one over to you. It's so very easy for someone to pick up your money box. They need be at your sale for only five minutes to know where you keep the money, and need only 15 seconds when your back is turned to pick it up and leave. Again we stress that most—almost all—people are as honest as you are. But some dishonest persons do circulate among us nice guys. Just be alert and you won't have to worry about them.

Remember to keep your doors to your house locked. Probably most of the family will be out in the garage or down in the basement or out on the lawn, or wherever, watching what's going on at the sale. So keep the doors locked so no one unintentionally, or intentionally for that matter, wanders into your house looking for the bathroom or whatever. You'll probably have someone come up and ask if there is a bathroom they can use. If you wish to have people use your bathroom facilities, have one of the extra co-workers accompany them inside, wait outside the door, and then accompany them back outside, carefully re-locking the door as they leave. If you want to avoid people in your home, tell them that the house is locked and you can't leave your post to unlock the door. If they persist, you'll either have to do as we suggest above, or tell them frankly that you cannot allow anyone in the house during your sale. Refer them to the nearest gas station or public facility.

Be sure that the chair at your cash station is never moved so that the person manning the cash box will be able to sit down at all times. This assures that they won't wander away to see something or to answer a question.

HOUSE KEYS. Let the keeper of the main cash box be the keeper of the house keys. Then if you or the other co-workers have to hurry to the bathroom, you won't have to go to four different people asking who has the key.

If someone comes to your sale and wants to pay for a 25¢ item with a $50 or $100 bill, tell them you don't have that kind of change and ask them to go down to the nearby retail store or open bank for change. There are many security reasons for this, probably not necessary to mention here. Also, you don't want to use up all your change. Just remember all the signs you've seen at gas stations which state that they won't accept large bills at night. It's sort of the same philosophy. People coming to garage sales should bring small bills. If they come with only big bills to buy small items, they either were not thinking (and I'm being kind), or they have something else in mind. In either case, big bills are their problem, not yours, and you should not worry about a sale lost over failure to change a ridiculously large bill to pay for a small item.

Except for the person at the cash box, all workers should circulate at a garage sale. There are several reasons for this, not the least of which is for security purposes.

The last person customers pass as they leave is you, or whoever is at the cash box station. Keep a sharp eye as people leave. If someone is leaving with something that you haven't received payment for, call to them and ask them if you can help them. That's usually reminder enough for them to come over and pay you. If they say they've already paid and you know darn well they haven't, say, wow, that's strange because whoever took their money didn't record it in the book (as you glance into your record book—which won't really give that information, but will appear to). It's up to you if you want to make an issue of someone's taking something without paying after you have used every nice method to remind them to pay. Of course it is embarrassing to have a scene at your sale. You could ask someone to be at your sale just to take care of this situation, but it shouldn't be necessary, because more than likely it will not happen. You have taken the most obvious security measures by constantly guarding the cash box and by having the coworkers walk around the sale area to keep an eye on what's going on. All the things you're selling are items that you don't want or need, or they wouldn't be for sale. So it's up to you whether you want to pursue this kind of happening. It's probably more a matter of principle than anything else.

In summary, if you are sure that someone has taken something, on purpose, without paying, call them on it as discussed above. If they don't respond as they should, let them go. But call over a co-worker and ask him/her to walk casually out to the street and make note of this person's license number. Then call the police. At least you'll feel that you are not being taken advantage of—even for that horrible vase you'd always hated.

Chapter Eleven

Customer Relations

The most important thing about working with your customers is—don't hover. You'll know if someone wants you. They'll look for you—and you'll be easily recognizable because of your apron, or hat, or badge. You will also know if they want to chat. That's half the fun of a garage sale, getting to meet all kinds of wonderful people. Do take time and enjoy your customers.

Don't be pushy. Of the thousands of people who love to attend garage sales, there aren't two who like to be pressured into buying something. Leave your customers alone to pick and choose. Chat about the weather, stock market conditions, or who will take the World Series next year. But don't push something on someone who doesn't want it. Someone else will want that very item, and you won't have to push them at all. Then everyone will be happy—the person who didn't want it, the person who did, and best of all, you.

Have a pep talk with your co-workers before the sale starts. Remind them that some folks are going to criticize items or their prices, or both. That seems to be part of the garage sale game for some garage sale-ers, so don't be offended. They are really just doing it for the sport. (Some sport.) You'll also hear remarks like "they don't have *anything* at this sale!" What this really means is that you don't have the particular thing they've been looking for at seven other sales and haven't found yet. More comments, though, will be positive. Customer for customer, you will hear more nice things than negative.

Don't ever argue with a customer. If you are told something is overpriced, just smile and say you didn't realize it was not priced properly, but it belongs to someone else who isn't here right now. "Why not come back later in the day (or tomorrow or whenever you plan to reduce prices) because everything left unsold will be reduced in price." And since this item is overpriced, surely no one else will buy it and the purchase can be made when it's marked down. Say this nicely. Kill 'em with kindness. I know, I know. You're trying, but the person just won't die. Keep smiling.

If a dealer comes by and wants to purchase a group of things at a reduced price, you'd be better off not to sell. Ask the dealer to come back at the end of the sale and you will sell everything left over for a flat fee. Then do it. You'll have time before the dealer comes back to take out anything you've been having second thoughts about selling (which should be nothing). But it does give you a reprieve, just in case. Most dealers are very nice, but remember what they're doing. They are buying up things which they will take either to their booth at a flea market or to a thrift shop they own, and sell it at much more than you're selling it for. Or maybe they are planning to have their own garage sale. Don't be flim-flammed by them. Remember they're in the business of doing this every day. They will know every right thing to say to convince you to sell ahead of time. Unless you really want to sell things quickly and be done with your sale, hold fast. Tell them to come back when the sale is over. Don't let them be selective at the end of the sale. If they want it all, great. At least they'll haul everything away and you won't have to.

People want to dicker. It's in their blood. This is a fun part of garage sales for some people. If you want to dicker, fine, but you're opening a Pandora's box. Because if you dicker with one person, you'll have to dicker with anyone else who sees you dealing. It will spread and spread until it becomes unmanageable. Remember that you spent a good deal of time pricing things at an amount you felt was reasonable. Trust your judgment. Who is to say you're wrong? If someone wants to deal on an item, again, point to your sign which says "Saturday at 4 p.m. (or "all day Sunday") every item left unsold will be reduced in price. Everything must be sold!" and tell them to come back and get the deal of the century. If they really want the item, they'll buy it at the price you have marked. If they truly feel you're out of line in your pricing, but still want the item, you have given them the opportunity to come back when you reduce prices. You will not lose many sales by this method. Keep in mind that the customer has nothing to lose by asking you to reduce a price. You do.

Be sure to tell your co-workers to be absolutely honest with the customers. If the customer asks a question and you don't know the answer, such as "How old is this mixer?", tell them you don't know. Those are three very hard words for a lot of us to say. Then point out the person who owns the mixer and let that person tell the customer all about the mixer.

We've sold a lot of things we really could not remember the age of, or quite frankly did not know how much it cost. You can probably remember the item's being around the house for over a year, or maybe someone gave it to you three summers ago. Don't try to make an item younger than it is. Of course, don't make it older, either. Just be honest. If you are really in the dark about how much you paid for something way back when, tell your customer that because you didn't remember the cost, you looked in a Sears catalogue for a similar item and priced yours accordingly, reducing it to garage sale prices. Because that is what you did do, or should have done if you were in doubt. Almost everyone trusts the Sears catalogue. Have your copy available under your cash station table. You can always grab it out and use it for reference if you feel it is necessary. But for the most part, you will find that it won't be necessary.

Chapter Twelve

Actual Sale Day(s)

You will probably recall that in all three examples of garage sale ads we included in an earlier section, we noted that the starting time of the sale would be 10 a.m. There is a very good reason for this. If you say 10 a.m., the people will come at 9 a.m. If you say 9 a.m., they will come at 8 a.m. At one "9 a.m. start" porch sale we held, we got up very early the day of the sale, actually at 6 a.m., to put the finishing touches on items and set out those we'd kept inside. The moment we turned on the porch light so we could see what we were doing, people started to come. And the only reason we had to turn on the light was because the sun wasn't up yet. The customers were, though. If you really want your sale to start at 8 a.m., make your starting time 9 a.m. Trust me, trust me. This is unfailingly true. One of the funniest garage sale ads we've ever read started out "Garage Sale 8 a.m. til 5 p.m. No early birds . . . (it went on about what they were selling, and ended) . . . Remember, no early birds!" If the unlikely should occur and folks really don't come to your sale before opening time (neee-ver happen), you can use the time for last minute things, like a nice cup of coffee.

The reason people come early to your sale is to snap up all your bargains. This is when the weekend bargainers and flea market dealers come, too. Don't dicker with them. Tell them very politely that the price is "as marked." They'll try every trick in the book to get you to sell an item at less than it's marked. They'll tell you that the item is in terrible shape and they'll give you 25¢ (or whatever) for it and no more. Your retort, if you feel feisty, might be "Then why in the world would you want to buy such a piece of junk?" They'll tell you that you don't know a thing about the value of things. Maybe they're right, but this is your sale. Don't give in. This is early on the first day of your sale, so give the other customers coming later in the day a chance at the item at the price you have marked it.

Stop right here. We have a suggestion that you have heard us alluding to in earlier sections, and which you may or may not wish to take. If you are having a three-day sale, post a sign saying "All items remaining unsold on Sunday will be drastically reduced until EVERYTHING is sold!" If you are having a two-day sale, state on your sign that price reductions will begin at (whatever time) on the last day. If you are having a one-day sale, have your sign read "At 4 p.m., all items remaining will be drastically reduced in price." A real advantage to a three-day sale is that Saturday night, after everyone has gone, you can remove those items which you were willing to sell at what you thought they were worth, but don't want to reduce. Save these items for your next sale. The other items, however, you really do want to be rid of, and this is the way to do it. If someone truly wants an item, they will not wait until the last day to buy it at a reduced price. They will be afraid that the item will be sold before then, and it probably will be. But if there is some crazy thing that they would be willing to pay $2 for but not $5, they'll come back just to see what you've reduced it to. As the day goes on, keep reducing the prices until you have sold (or given away if you care to) every blessed thing you put out. Remember that if it's really "junk" to you and you really want to be rid of it, if you don't sell it, you'll just have to pay to have the remains hauled off.

You may have thought that you'd donate the leftovers to some charitable organization. Do them a favor and don't. If it's so bad that no one bought it, even at your reduced prices, it's not worth the organization's time to sort through it. This does not apply to clothing, however, which, if it does not sell well at your sale, can be used by organizations who help the poor. Give all your leftover clothes to someone, providing they are decent and clean (the clothes, that is). But we know they'd be clean or you wouldn't have put them in your sale. Right?

Chapter Thirteen

Very Unlikely Events

Very unlikely events are very unlikely to happen. However, if they should happen, which is very unlikely, you'd better know what to do.

For instance, a customer strolls over to look at your sewing center items, trips over a table leg and falls flat on her face. Result: broken tooth. Of course you will rush to her assistance (we hope this will not be the person from the cash box station) and make her comfortable, find out if she wants to call someone. In other words, do everything you can to help her and make her feel better. Get her name and address. Also get the names and addresses of witnesses, if there were any, but DO NOT make an issue of getting witnesses. Probably either you or one of the other workers saw what happened. Take care of her immediate needs, but go on with your sale. If she is alone and needs assistance to get somewhere, have her call someone to come for her. If she has no one, you may suggest that one of the co-workers take her home, and she can pick up her car later when her family or friends are available. Get everything back to normal as quickly as possible without seeming unfeeling. But do get back to normal quickly.

Did you know that, should this person who had an accident at your garage sale, make a claim against you for damages, most likely your homeowner's insurance (liability coverage) will cover the claim? However, on behalf of your insurance company, let me take this opportunity to tell you not to volunteer this information. If she calls you later and tells you that you are responsible for her accident and you must pay her medical bills and all, simply tell her you will be in touch with her very soon. Then immediately call your insurance agent and state what happened. The insurance company will handle the rest of it for you.

Or, for instance, two cars collide while trying to maneuver out of your driveway. There is no traffic code to cover this, because it happened on private property. Normally, the problem is handled between the two drivers. The police would be called if there were extensive damage to either car, or if someone were hurt. It would not be out of line to report this kind of occurrence to your insurance company in the event one of the drivers attempts to involve you because the accident happened on your property. Again, if you are liable, you probably have coverage through your homeowner's liability coverage. Check with your agent.

A very small group of people in our country have become "sue crazy," and look for every opportunity to get fast and easy money through the courts. If anyone attempts to make any kind of claim against you, say nothing and contact your insurance company. And then, if necessary, contact your attorney. Don't try to handle it yourself. And keep your mouth closed!

Another very unlikely event, we hope, would be a wild child racing around your sale area playing havoc with your wares and causing general disruption of your sale. We would hope that the parents would notice and control the child, but often they get so absorbed in their shopping, they shut everything else out of their minds. First step is to gently tell the child please to slow down and be a little quiet so that the older folks can hear. If that doesn't work, you might suggest to the little one that if he or she doesn't settle down, you will just have to tell the mother or father about the bad behavior. If this doesn't work, do tell mom or dad. Tell them that you're afraid that the little one is going to get hurt and perhaps they would like to hold the child's hand for safety. If they don't get the hint from this, you'll have to decide how far you want to go. If the child is really disrupting everyone, you may have to ask them to leave. That's pretty harsh and "an unlikely event," but it could happen. Just think about what you'd do in advance, and should it occur, you won't be floored by the situation.

The unlikely event of theft at your garage sale is covered in the SECURITY section of this book.

Chapter Fourteen

General Hints

There are two schools of thought regarding rearranging stock as it is depleted. One is, if things are sold, don't fill in the spaces from which the items were removed, because it indicates to other customers that things are moving and therefore these must be good bargains. The other is, keep your display area neat and stretch the remaining items into bare spaces. That way no one will think that things are dreadfully picked over and all the good bargains are gone. In reality, "all the good bargains" are simply what a particular customer wants. So you're never out of bargains. The old expression "one person's trash is another's treasure" is overused for good reason. It is quite true. We love the little picture frames we picked up for 25¢ each at a garage sale. They were there late in the afternoon on the last day of the sale, so we must have been the only ones who liked or needed them. So there you are.

If you want the merchandise rearranged from time to time to "stretch" in the display areas, ask your co-workers to do it when there is a lull in customers. This will happen frequently during the day. But beware when this happens, because after about 15 minutes, they will seem to come in hordes. At garage sales, due to some unknown phenomenon, customers seem to come in groups. They don't come in nice, even numbers throughout the day. So be prepared for the mass entrance—and the mass exodus. A group of customers who arrive all at the same time, even though they have no connection and never saw one another before, all seem to leave at the same time. It seems that when one person leaves, the others follow. So keep everyone chatting and looking, and they'll stay and buy more.

If you close early, you will miss people who couldn't get there until just about closing time. Dusk will automatically end your sale. People stop coming then, so 6 o'clock is usually a safe time to close up for the day. Hang up your "Closed" sign. Tuck away your outside items, close up and regroup for the next day's session. If "next day" is your drastically-reduced-price day, you may want to physically mark the lowered prices. However, this isn't necessary. Just hang up your "All Prices Reduced" sign and your "25% off Every Item!" sign and you're all set.

Remember about the refreshment stand. If your sale is longer than one day, whoever is running the stand will have to prepare more goodies for the next morning. Don't forget to see that the coffee pot is cleaned and all dirty cups and napkins are picked up.

Straighten the entire area the night before and you won't have to face the mess in the morning.

If you're tired and shot down, gather your co-workers around the kitchen table (if you didn't sell it), break out a bottle of wine—or a bottle of soda—and count the loot. That'll do wonders to perk you right up.

Get a good night's rest—ready for the next day.

Chapter Fifteen

Two-Family Garage Sales

At times, you may not have enough merchandise to make a good garage sale possible, but if you combine your stuff with your neighbor's wares, you'll have material for a really good-sized sale. Having a two-family sale has other advantages. It allows you to split the costs of advertising in the newspaper, the cost of supplies to make signs, etc. It automatically gives you extra workers who must be there, rather than workers you asked to come over and help. They will have a vested interest in this sale. That interest is profits. There will be help in preparation of the items for selling, help in pricing, help in set-up and in clean-up. There will be more ideas floating around.

One word of caution. Pick the family carefully. Are you sure that you can count on them to be there if the sale is being held at your house, and not leave to run their own personal errands? Will they help and really pitch in with the dirty work? Do they agree to keep little kids and pets out of the way, and do both participants agree on general guidelines for the sale? If the answer to every one of these questions is yes, proceed with your two-family sale.

When everything is straight as to who is going to do what and when, jot it down so that later on you can refer to the schedule which will tell you that Millie is at the cash box from 10 til 12, then you relieve her. Billy and Joey work the refreshment stand in hour shifts. Both can be there during the hour, but one of them must be there check the schedule to see who is supposed to be there.

It would not be worth any amount of increased profits at your sale if, because of some misunderstanding, you lost the friendship of good neighbors. Just remember to give two-family garage sales a lot of thought and planning.

In order to be sure that each family gets its proper profits from their own merchandise, when you go shopping for stick-on labels, get two different colors. You may have to go to an office supply store in order to get colored labels. Then, for instance, all blue labels belong to your family, all yellow labels belong to the neighbor's family. When the item is being paid for and you remove the label for your record book, you will put all yellow labels on one page and all blue labels on another. The labels themselves will have on them the amount of money that each item brought in. There can be no mix-up in profits as long as you know that your items had your color labels on them and your neighbor's items had their color labels on them.

Be sure to keep a separate page when you begin to reduce prices (see RECORD KEEPING). You will stick the label in the book, but beside it, you will note in ink what the item really sold for at the reduced price.

Two-family sales make it absolutely necessary for accurate record keeping. If you're having a sale all by yourself, you might not be too worried about how much you spent for this or that, but when others are involved, you'll feel much better about everything if you both present receipts for all supplies and services to be used in the final tally of profits. Be sure both sides agree on what any helpers are paid. This will be kids, we would think. You don't want to promise the necessary helpers $10.00 each for moving furniture for you and then find that the family giving the sale with you feels that is too much. Agree on all expenditures before they are made. You'll stay friends, and besides, that's the proper way to do it.

If you feel uneasy about having a two-family sale because you can't bring yourself to discuss prior agreements and arrangements with them, have them read this book. They'll understand what you're trying to do.

Regarding fairness in a two-family sale, you may have to put up with all the aggravation of actually having the sale at your house, but your neighbors will have to haul all their stuff over to your house. That's a lot of work, too. If you feel you should get a bigger cut than just the profits from your items because you are having the sale at your house, bring this out before you even begin to plan the sale. Remember that it is advantageous to have the other family join you in your sale because you will have more items to offer, which will always draw and keep and larger crowd. Few people spend more than 10 minutes at a tiny garage sale. They usually feel it's not worth their time. And they're probably right. So it may be that another family joining you in the sale is more of an advantage to you than the disadvantage of having the sale at your house.

Don't go along with the two-family garage sale harboring any secret resentments. This will be a fun experience for everyone and there is no place for hard feelings. Keep it light.

Three- or four- or more family sales become more complicated, simply because there are so many opinions flying around that no two people can agree on anything. We're against them.

We drove 40 miles to visit a "Four-Family Sale" which we thought would be a humdinger. When we got there at 11 a.m., there was no sign of a sale, although it was to have started at 8 a.m. We thought we might have misread the ad in the paper, but we had the paper with us, re-read the ad and knew we were there on the right day, well within the proper hours. Several other cars drove slowly by the house, obviously looking for the sale, so we weren't the only people disappointed. Bet your life the four families had a falling out over the sale and just decided at the last minute to call it off. What a shame.

Chapter Sixteen

Kids' Garage Sales

When you scavenged through your adolescents' rooms, did they scream and holler? If so, and because you're grabbing their own private property, why not let them have their own private sale? If they are enthusiastic about this suggestion, stack up all they have to sell and decide if it's enough for their own sale. If not, like a two-family garage sale, they may want to ask their best friend to join them with all their unneeded, unwanted treasures. It is a lot of work for them, but if you coach them with the same rules and regulations as we've talked about for a standard garage sale, they'll be just as successful. Here is one where we definitely suggest a one-day sale.

If they don't have enough stuff of their own, and don't want to involve other kids but still feel entitled to make the profits from the sale of their own things, let them have their own booth at your sale. Either rent them the booth, if you're doing all the preparatory work such as advertising, sign making, etc., or have them help, dirty work and all, in setting up the entire sale. Rent could be a percentage of their profits, or, if they have enough items to warrant it, a nominal rental fee of $5 or $10, or whatever.

Keep it on a business-like basis. Don't let them weasel out of any part of the deal, whether it be joining you in your sale or holding their own. Don't do their work for them. Let them realize the immeasurable pleasure of achieving something on their own—something no one ever thought they could do by themselves. It will be one of the better lessons in life they've been allowed to experience so far.

A child the age of 12 will not be able to handle a sale of his own, but possibly could run his own booth. Fourteen and up usually hits the right age for their own private sale.

One thing you will have to do is be sure that, in their enthusiasm to make money, they are not offering for sale the new designer jeans you just had a heart attack paying for, or their bed and dresser, or their baby brother. They will give you very rational reasons why these very items should be sold, but hold fast. The jeans are not yet out of style (since last week), you do not plan to buy them a new bedroom set, and their baby brother will grow up some day and they're bound to like him better then.

If they don't prepare properly or put enough work and effort into their sale, let them fail. This may, in the long run, profit them more than the proceeds of the sale.

Chapter Seventeen

Garage Sales as a Business

You've just hung out your "closed" sign for the last time, you're tired but still smiling. You had fun, achieved your purpose of disposing of things you didn't want or need, but most of all, you've made money—much more than you ever thought you could. It was a lot of work, but worth it. Would you do it again? Soon? You might want to consider what many suburbanites are going into these days—garage sales as a business. It can be a real moneymaker.

If you have an ample place to store things, a little extra money to buy merchandise, and determination, you can be in the business quickly. You do this by attending other people's garage sales, buying up things cheaply, cleaning them up, displaying them properly, and selling them at twice what you paid for them. Remember when we talked about the dealer who tries to buy your things at a low price? That's what we mean. There is only one trick to this. You must be able to pick the sleepers at other sales—things that you can visualize in better condition, all cleaned up. If you buy duds at other people's sales, they will still be duds at yours. Remember the items that sold best at your sale and buy these kinds of things. You can quickly see the possibilities of this by visiting half a dozen garage sales with your business in mind.

If you do decide to try this business, ask a friend to join you as a partner. It is much more fun with two people working together and collaborating.

You may want to plan a sale once a month, or once every three months. If you run this kind of business on any kind of regular basis, you may need a license, even though for the casual garage sale, there was no such necessity. You'll have to check into the sales tax situation, too. Also, if you live in a zoned area, you may be prohibited from carrying on a business from your home. Spend the time to check these things out before you invest any more of your time, and especially before you invest any money.

You will also need an extension of your insurance coverage on your home to cover "doing business from the home."

The best location for starting this kind of business is semirural, where you cannot possibly offend your neighbors, even if there are no zoning restrictions. You certainly would not want to end a long-established, good relationship with your neighbor by starting a business, no matter how legal it is, which infringes on your neighbor's rights by virtue of tying up the street, possibly having folks tramp across the lawn to reach your sale, or causes any unreasonable inconvenience. However, if your place is out in the country, easy to get to, and with lots of land around, you have the exact location to hold garage sales on a regular basis. That great empty barn we talked about earlier is the absolute best.

As you become more adept at selecting bargains, you may become interested in keeping an eye out for valuable merchandise offered for sale as junk. Only one buy of this kind and you're hooked. Spend a few afternoons in your library, going through basic antique collecting books and you will realize that everyone who collects antiques and valuables starts at the beginning just like you.

There are several good books in the library for beginners which you will want to read. There are many to select from that will give you a start in the right direction.

Chapter Eighteen

Garage Sales for Charity

Since garage sales are becoming so popular, when it comes time to collect sale items from your church group or members of your organization for your big fund raiser of the year, you may find that no one has anything much left. They've all had garage sales of their own.

In order to be successful, you have got to let your people know well in advance that your organization is planning a sale, and they should start saving everything for you. You must line up a storage space, because many people will tell you that if you take it now, you can have it. Otherwise they will have to get rid of it. You should use at least a three-month lead time for this kind of sale to assure that you accumulate enough items to make it worthwhile.

One thing to remember, however, is that you have 100% profit for your organization with a garage sale. Those who help will donate their time; you will probably be able to use the church hall or the meeting place of your organization, or if there is none available, someone within the organization will probably allow you to use their extra large garage. So, other than advertising, which is often free to a charitable organization, everything you make will be clear profit. So it is really worth the time and effort.

Follow the general guidelines set out for a private garage sale and you can't go wrong. The refreshment stand at a charity sale is terrific. It turns into a bake sale with a built-in clientele. Schedule people to bring freshly baked goodies throughout the day, all day, on each day of your sale.

A church in one area of the country where we lived had a novel twist on the garage sale gambit. Once a year they invited everyone in their town to bring their items to the church to be sold at a garage sale. The person bringing in the item for sale at the event advised the garage sale committee (who were very experienced at this by now) what they felt should be charged for their item. If the committee felt the suggested selling price was too high or too low, they helped the person come to a more realistic price.

The church then sold all the items at their sale and gave 50% of the proceeds to the person who brought in the item and kept 50% of the proceeds. Participation in the sale was not limited to church members only. Everyone in the community was welcome to participate. But the garage sale committee did all the work.

There were strict rules, however, for any item to be sold at their sale. Everything had to be shining clean and in excellent condition. Items such as children's coats, women's wool dresses, etc., had to be dry-cleaned (dry cleaning bill still attached!) before they would be considered for the sale. This assured that everything offered for sale was a tremendous bargain without doubt. And everyone knew it.

This was such a successful idea that it was held yearly, and everyone in the community and then some flocked to the sale because they knew everything there was worth buying.

It netted a lot of money—no overhead. It allowed people to sell their unneeded items without the bother of having their own sale. Everyone won.

If you try this, have your most organized member set up the bookkeeping, because it is much more involved than a regular garage sale. But no one minds, because it is so profitable.

Chapter Nineteen

Record Keeping

It is necessary to keep only two kinds of records for your garage sale: receipts and expenditures. We suggest keeping your records in a thin spiral notebook, 8 x 10 ½, wide-lined. We suggest "thin" because this will prevent you from using it for another project later on and then throwing it away, losing all that valuable information you have accumulated for your next sale.

EXPENDITURES

You will need three columns to keep track of expenditures—date, item and cost. The date column is self-explanatory, the date on which you actually purchased the item. Item should be definite enough so that next time you hold a sale, you'll be able to decipher what you bought. Add where you purchased it, too, for future reference. Cost, also, is self-explanatory. Include the tax so you will have a true total cost.

If you are having a two-family sale, add the family name of who purchased and paid for an item so you can give credit for these expenditures in the final tally of profits.

RECEIPTS

These are the pages on which you will stick the labels which you have removed from the item when someone at your sale purchased it. The only time this will vary is if you have a two-family sale. You may wish to keep separate pages for each family, but this really is not necessary because the color of the label will tell you whose sale it was.

Be sure to start a new "Receipts" page when you begin reducing prices. On the reduced price page, you will have to allow space for the label and room next to the label to indicate the price at which the item finally sold.

ITEM NUMBERS

We talked about "item numbers" in the PRICING section. Your stick-on label would read: 0001 – 25¢.

As part of your record keeping, if you choose to do this, you will have a list of every item you are selling, with its item number and cost. If a person hands you a pie plate they have selected to buy, and the item number of the label says 0034, you refer to your list. You may find that 0034 is a coffee pot, and you know the label has been switched. If the price is also marked on the item in chalk, you will have no problem completing this sale. You just tell the person that somehow someone must have switched the labels and the correct price is what has been marked in chalk on the item.

A numbering, or item number, system is very good for a two or more family sale. Use a four-digit code, the first number indicating which family owned the piece being sold. That would mean that item 1006 belongs to the family designated "1," the first number. The number 2010 means the item belongs to the family designated "2." The last three numbers are usually plenty to give each item in your sale a different number. That means 999 items for each family. If you have more than 999 items, you probably should not include another family in your sale. You have enough yourself.

UN-TAGGED ITEMS

Don't forget to have a page with a listing of the items that you did not label, along with the prices you have determined for them. This will include those 45 miscellaneous knives, forks and spoons that you are selling for 10¢ each but did not want to waste labels on. The price each is on a sign above the items. The same price is listed in your book.

Chapter Twenty

Hints for Garage Sale Shoppers

Very obviously, if you want to get the "bargains," get up and get there on time. Anything you want or need is your "bargain" but you'll surely have more to look at if you get there on time. Don't go too early, though, because if whoever is holding the garage sale reads this book, you'll just end up sitting in your car for an hour. If you think you must go early, take a magazine with you to read while you wait for the proper starting time.

If you feel an item is terribly overpriced, and there is no sign stating that items will be reduced at the end of the sale, ask. Perhaps the person holding the sale hadn't thought of that and he/she will tell you to come back later and if it hasn't been sold, they'll knock off a few dollars.

Don't make fun of an item, or tell the seller how bad it is, hoping to get a lower price. That's rude, and you'll just make the person mad and you'll never get it. Be as pleasant to the seller as you hope the seller will be to you and you'll get a lot further with bargaining. If the seller says the price is firm on an item, don't push. The seller means it.

Be on the lookout for bargains such as old bottles (old Avon bottles are now collector's pieces!). Many times they are just thrown in because they've been around littering up the house for so long. This is where the fun begins. You might hit on something great. But don't buy on speculation unless it is so cheap you can't resist it and have absolutely nothing else to do with your money.

When checking out clothing at a sale, look it over carefully. Although a dress may be something you'd never think of wearing, it might have a belt that will go exactly with another outfit you have. Have you priced belts at your better department stores lately?

Appliqués on children's clothing may be salvageable even though the article of clothing itself is not. Very expensive T-shirts from

Disney World have Disney characters appliqued on them. The child wears out the T-shirt, so it's in the sale. Buy it, remove the appliqué and sew it on a new T-shirt that fits your little one. These Disney appliqués, in particular, are excellent; they never fade and after many washings are as bright and colorful as the day they were new. They will outlast many T-shirts to which they're sewn.

An old toaster, broken and in total disrepair, may have a knob on it just like the one that is missing from your toaster at home. You haven't been able to get a new one for yours because they don't make that model any more, but other than that, your toaster is fine. If you can buy the broken toaster for almost nothing, you're getting a real bargain. You've been able to put your own toaster back to looking like new with all its knobs matching. The same applies to any old appliances with knobs, buttons, or even shelves that you might need.

So look beyond the item itself at the possibilities that aren't apparent to everyone. But always remember—let the buyer beware. That means you. If you get a lemon, don't despair. You probably didn't spend much on it anyway.

And in Conclusion . . .

Your sale is now over and you feel that you would like to be able to repay all the people who helped you with it. You will find that no one except the kids will accept money. We suggest a picnic or dinner to say thank you to these great friends. At the end of this celebration party, you might feel constrained to stand up and announce that since everyone was so nice to help you, you'll be glad to give a hand when any of them has a garage sale of their own. But be prepared to hear these words reverberating back into your ears some day in the not too distant future, because we'll bet everyone who helped you with your sale will want to have one just as successful as yours.

In closing we want to tell you a little story which really happened just like this . . .

The college daughter we talked about earlier in this book attends University of Texas in Austin, Texas. She is involved in a work/study program in which she spends every other semester working in the engineering department of a General Motors facility up north. Last year, we drove up in her car to help her get settled into an apartment she was renting during her stay at General Motors. The apartment lacked a few things, so we jumped into her car and went off garage sale-ing to see if we could find what she needed. At one sale, we chatted with two ladies who told us that they had hit 16 sales already that day. They were, they told us, real garage sale enthusiasts. We walked out with them as they left and came to our car first. They were astonished when they saw our Texas license plates. "Boy, you two really must enjoy going to garage sales to come all that distance!" We just smiled.

PILOT BOOKS READING SHELF

PROFITABLE PART-TIME, HOME BASED BUSINESSES. Shows how to make additional money from a part-time business requiring a slight investment. All the enterprises fulfill legitimate community needs. The amount of time and commitment required is flexible and may be expanded or retracted to fit the needs and abilities of the individual.

HOW TO START A SECRETARIAL AND BUSINESS SERVICE. A public secretarial service is one of the easiest businesses to start and successfully operate. This book tells you, step-by-step, how to get started. You learn about choosing the right location, advertising, obtaining clients, purchasing equipment and how to expand in other fields.

THE SENIOR CITIZEN'S 10-MINUTES-A-DAY FITNESS PLAN. No fancy equipment. No complicated exercises. No unnecessary exertion. This fitness plan is designed with an awareness of senior limitations and will improve muscle tone, promote cardiovascular health and stimulate blood flow. It also includes two dozen hidden exercises in everyday activities and discusses sensible eating patterns.

A WOMAN'S GUIDE TO STARTING A SMALL BUSINESS. Put your skills and experience to work. Shows what other women have accomplished by starting imaginative ventures and points out the many possibilities open to you. This book covers low-overhead businesses, evaluating your potential and finding business management assistance. It outlines the seven basic steps in setting up a business, plus a 20-point beginner's checklist.

THE FLEA MARKET ENTREPRENEUR. Shows you step-by-step how to get started and how to cash in. Covers what to sell, where to find merchandise, finding out about the shows, pricing, setting up your display and selling techniques. The final result, once you've learned the ropes, is a profitable small business of your own.

TRACING, CHARTING AND WRITING YOUR FAMILY HISTORY. Shows how interesting and simple it is to start a family history. You'll learn how and where to obtain records; how to compile a genealogical notebook; how to prepare a chart of your family and suggestions regarding reference sources. The more you get involved, the more fascinating the project becomes.

Pilot Books P.O. Box 2102, Greenport, NY 11944-2102